The NFL's Greatest Teams

DALLAS COWBOYS

Marcia Zappa

Big Buddy Books

An Imprint of Abdo Publishing
www.abdopublishing.com

www.abdopublishing.com

Published by Abdo Publishing, a division of ABDO, PO Box 398166, Minneapolis, Minnesota 55439.
Copyright © 2015 by Abdo Consulting Group, Inc. International copyrights reserved in all countries. No part
of this book may be reproduced in any form without written permission from the publisher. Big Buddy Books™
is a trademark and logo of Abdo Publishing.

Printed in the United States of America, North Mankato, Minnesota.
042014
092014

Cover Photo: ASSOCIATED PRESS.
Interior Photos: ASSOCIATED PRESS (pp. 5, 7, 11, 14, 15, 17, 18, 19, 20, 21, 23, 25, 27, 28, 29); Getty Images
    (p. 9); Sports Illustrated/Getty Images (pp. 9, 13).

Coordinating Series Editor: Rochelle Baltzer
Contributing Editors: Bridget O'Brien, Sarah Tieck
Graphic Design: Michelle Labatt

Library of Congress Cataloging-in-Publication Data

Zappa, Marcia, 1985-
  Dallas Cowboys / Marcia Zappa.
     pages cm. -- (The NFL's greatest teams)
  ISBN 978-1-62403-360-5
1. Dallas Cowboys (Football team)--Juvenile literature. I. Title.
  GV956.D3Z36 2014
  796.332'647642812--dc23
                            2013046913

Contents

A Winning Team

The Dallas Cowboys are a football team from Dallas, Texas. They have played in the National Football League (NFL) for more than 50 years.

The Cowboys have had good seasons and bad. But time and again, they've proven themselves. Let's see what makes the Cowboys one of the NFL's greatest teams.

Dark blue, silver, and white are the team's colors.

League Play

The NFL got its start in 1920. Its teams have changed over the years. Today, there are 32 teams. They make up two conferences and eight divisions.

The Cowboys play in the East Division of the National Football Conference (NFC). This division also includes the New York Giants, the Philadelphia Eagles, and the Washington Redskins.

Team Standings

The NFC and the American Football Conference (AFC) make up the NFL. Each conference has a north, south, east, and west division.

The Redskins are a major rival of the Cowboys. Fans get excited when they face off!

Kicking Off

The Dallas Cowboys became a team in 1960. They missed the **draft** their first year. So, they got off to a hard start. The team had losing records for their first six seasons.

In 1966, things started looking up. In fact, the Cowboys quickly became one of the top NFL teams.

Penalty!

At first, the Cowboys were called the Steers. Then, they became the Rangers. But, there was already a baseball team in Dallas called the Rangers. So, they settled on the Cowboys as the team name.

The Cowboys didn't win a single game their first season.

Between 1966 and 1985, the Cowboys had 20 winning seasons in a row. This set an NFL record!

Highlight Reel

Between 1966 and 1985, the Cowboys made it to the Super Bowl five times. Their first Super Bowl was in 1971. Sadly, they lost at the last second to the Baltimore Colts 16–13.

The next year, the Cowboys won the Super Bowl! They beat the Miami Dolphins 24–3. The Cowboys won the Super Bowl again in 1978. They beat the Denver Broncos 27–10.

Roger Staubach (*number 12*) helped the Cowboys win the 1972 Super Bowl.

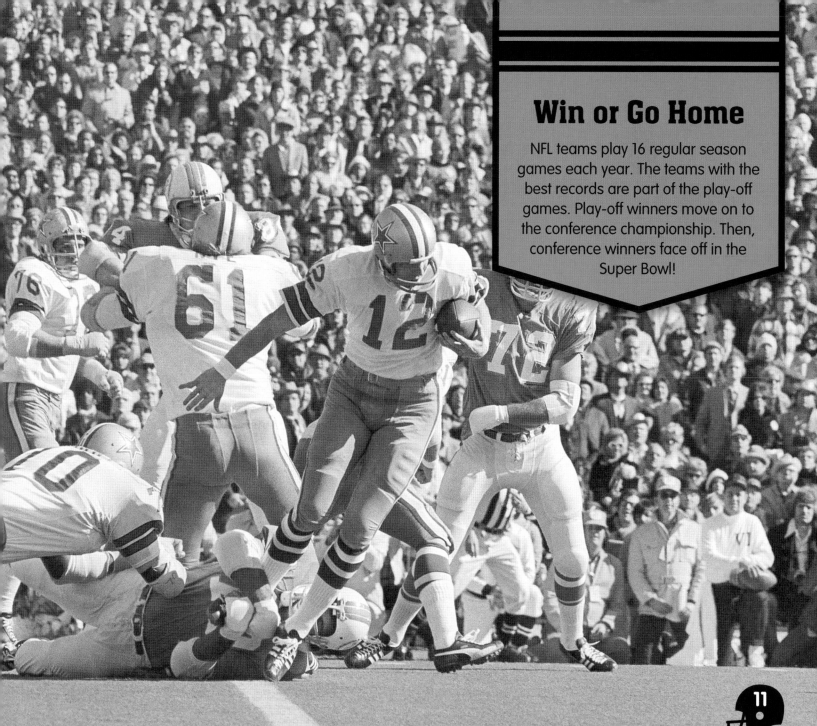

Win or Go Home

NFL teams play 16 regular season games each year. The teams with the best records are part of the play-off games. Play-off winners move on to the conference championship. Then, conference winners face off in the Super Bowl!

In 1989, the Cowboys got the first pick in the NFL **draft**. They chose quarterback Troy Aikman. He led the team to three Super Bowl wins in 1993, 1994, and 1996!

The Cowboys made the play-offs four times in the 2000s. But, they didn't make it back to the Super Bowl.

In 1996, the Cowboys became only the second NFL team to have won five Super Bowls!

13

Halftime! Stat Break

Pro Football Hall of Famers & Their Years with the Cowboys

Troy Aikman, Quarterback (1989–2000)
Larry Allen, Guard/Tackle (1994–2005)
Tony Dorsett, Running Back (1977–1987)
Bob Hayes, Wide Receiver (1965–1974)
Michael Irvin, Wide Receiver (1988–1999)
Bob Lilly, Defensive Tackle (1961–1974)
Mel Renfro, Cornerback/Safety (1964–1977)
Deion Sanders, Cornerback (1995–1999)
Tex Schramm, Contributor (1960–1989)
Emmitt Smith, Running Back (1990–2002)
Roger Staubach, Quarterback (1969–1979)
Randy White, Defensive Tackle (1975–1988)
Rayfield Wright, Offensive Tackle (1967–1979)

Fan Fun

NICKNAMES: America's Team, The Boys
STADIUM: AT&T Stadium
LOCATION: Arlington, Texas
MASCOT: Rowdy

Team Records

RUSHING YARDS
Career: Emmitt Smith, 17,162 yards (1990–2002)
Single Season: Emmitt Smith, 1,773 yards (1995)
PASSING YARDS
Career: Troy Aikman, 32,942 yards (1989–2000)
Single Season: Tony Romo, 4,903 yards (2012)
RECEPTIONS
Career: Jason Witten, 879 receptions and
    gaining (2003–)
Single Season: Michael Irvin, 111 receptions (1995)
ALL-TIME LEADING SCORER
Emmitt Smith, 986 points (1990–2002)

Famous Coaches

Tom Landry (1960–1988)
Jimmy Johnson (1989–1993)

Championships

SUPER BOWL APPEARANCES: **SUPER BOWL WINS**:
1971, 1972, 1976, 1978, 1979,   1972, 1978, 1993, 1994, 1996
1993, 1994, 1996

Coaches' Corner

Texas native Tom Landry coached the Cowboys for 29 years. He became the team's first coach in 1960. With Landry, the Cowboys won 270 games and two Super Bowls!

When Jerry Jones bought the Cowboys in 1989, he hired a new coach. Jimmy Johnson coached the team for five seasons. The Cowboys won back-to-back Super Bowls during Johnson's last two years.

D-▦

Landry created two new types of defenses. They are the 4-3 and the flex.

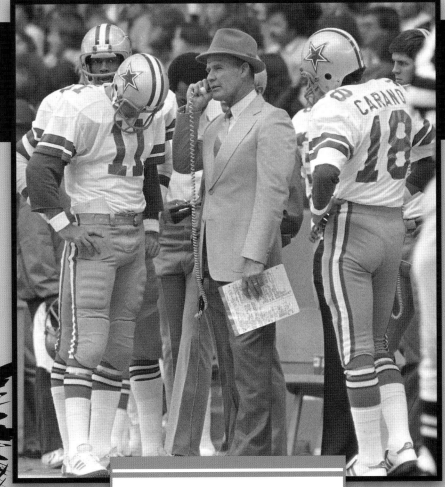

Landry was known for wearing suits and fancy hats called fedoras.

Jason Garrett became the team's coach in 2010.

Star Players

Bob Lilly DEFENSIVE TACKLE (1961–1974)

Bob Lilly was the first player ever **drafted** by the Cowboys. In 1972, he helped the team win its first Super Bowl. During Lilly's 14 years with the Cowboys, he only missed one game!

Roger Staubach QUARTERBACK (1969–1979)

Roger Staubach helped the Cowboys come back to win after being down in the fourth quarter 23 times! He became known as "Captain Comeback." He was named the Super Bowl's Most Valuable Player (MVP) in 1972.

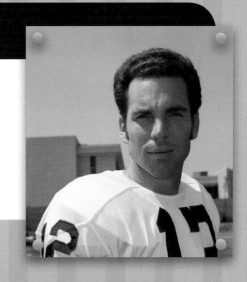

Tony Dorsett RUNNING BACK (1977–1987)

The Cowboys chose Tony Dorsett first in the 1977 **draft**. In 1983, he broke an NFL record by rushing 99 yards for a touchdown. When he **retired** in 1988, Dorsett had 12,739 rushing yards. That was the second most in the NFL!

Michael Irvin WIDE RECEIVER (1988–1999)

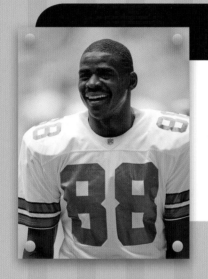

Michael Irvin was the top receiver for the Cowboys for eight seasons in a row. He helped the team win Super Bowls in 1993, 1994, and 1996. When he **retired**, Irvin had 750 receptions for 11,904 yards. This was more yards than any other Cowboy!

Troy Aikman QUARTERBACK (1989–2000)

Troy Aikman was **drafted** by the Cowboys as the first pick in 1989. He led the team to three Super Bowl wins. When he retired in 2000, Aikman had thrown for 32,942 yards. And, he had 165 touchdown passes. Both were team records!

Emmitt Smith RUNNING BACK (1990–2002)

Emmitt Smith has scored more points than any other Cowboy. During his time with the team, he scored 986 points. Smith helped the team win three Super Bowls. In 2002, he broke the NFL record for **career** rushing yards. By the time he **retired**, he had rushed for 18,355 yards!

Tony Romo QUARTERBACK (2003–)

Tony Romo joined the team in 2003. He became the starting quarterback in 2006. The next season, Romo helped the Cowboys win their division for the first time in 9 years. In 2009, he led the team to their first play-off win in 13 years!

AT&T Stadium

The Cowboys play home games at AT&T Stadium. It is in a **suburb** of Dallas called Arlington. AT&T Stadium opened in 2009. It can hold up to 100,000 people!

AT&T Stadium is known for its roof. It can open on nice days and close during bad weather.

Check the Replay

When it was built, AT&T Stadium had the world's largest HDTV!

America's Team

By the 1970s, the Cowboys were popular across the country! They became known as America's Team. Fans bought Cowboys clothing and **merchandise**.

In 1996, the team got a cowboy **mascot**. Rowdy wears a football uniform with cowboy boots and a giant cowboy hat. He goes to home games to help fans cheer on their team.

Rowdy rides around AT&T Stadium on a four-wheeler.

Final Call

The Cowboys have a long, rich history. The 1970s and 1990s saw many winning seasons and **championships**.

Even during losing seasons, true fans have stuck by them. Many believe that the Dallas Cowboys will remain one of the greatest teams in the NFL.

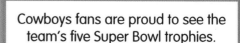

Cowboys fans are proud to see the team's five Super Bowl trophies.

Through the Years

1967
The team enters the play-offs for the first time.

1960
The Dallas Cowboys become an NFL team.

1971
Texas Stadium opens in Irving. Before this, the Cowboys played at the Cotton Bowl Stadium in Dallas.

1972
The Cowboys win their first Super Bowl!

1979
The Cowboys play in their fifth Super Bowl. This sets an NFL record!

1989

Jerry Jones purchases the Dallas Cowboys. As their new owner, he makes many changes.

2002

Emmitt Smith breaks the NFL's career rushing yards record!

1980

Defensive tackle Bob Lilly joins the Pro Football Hall of Fame. He is the first member to play his whole **career** for the Cowboys.

1993 & 1994

The Cowboys beat the Buffalo Bills in the Super Bowl two years in a row.

2009

The Cowboys get a big new stadium. First called Cowboys Stadium, the name changed to AT&T Stadium in 2013.

Postgame Recap

1. Who was the first coach of the Dallas Cowboys?
   A. Jimmy Johnson   **B**. Jerry Jones   **C**. Tom Landry

2. What is the name of the stadium where the Cowboys play home games?
   A. Cowboys Stadium   **B**. AT&T Stadium   **C**. Texas Stadium

3. Where is the stadium located?
   A. Arlington, Texas   **B**. Dallas, Texas   **C**. Fort Worth, Texas

4. Name 3 of the 13 Cowboys in the Pro Football Hall of Fame.

5. Why did the Cowboys have a hard time winning during their first
   few seasons?
   A. Their star quarterback was injured.
   B. They missed the draft.
   C. They didn't have a head coach.

1. C. 2. B. 3. A. 4. See page 14 5. B.

Glossary

career work a person does to earn money for living.

championship a game, a match, or a race held to find a first-place winner.

draft a system for professional sports teams to choose new players. When a team drafts a player, they choose that player for their team.

mascot something to bring good luck and help cheer on a team.

merchandise (MUHR-chuhn-dize) goods that are bought and sold.

retire to give up one's job.

suburb a town, village, or community just outside a city.

Websites

To learn more about the NFL's Greatest Teams, visit **booklinks.abdopublishing.com**. These links are routinely monitored and updated to provide the most current information available.

Index